WHO GOT
THE
KEYS?

Building Generational Wealth
Through Real Estate

Donna J Rogers

R' Legacy Publishing

WHO GOT THE KEYS?
Building Generational Wealth Through Real Estate

Donna J Rogers
drogers@rlegacyrealty.com

ISBN: 978-0-578-66312-8
Printed in the USA
All rights reserved

Interior design by: Destined To Publish | 773-783-2981

Dedication

This book is dedicated to my parents, John and Donna Sr. Rogers, who passed me the keys to unlock my purpose – to empower others through education and real estate.

I love and appreciate you dearly.

Special Thanks

To my amazing teenage niece, Mia Rogers,
thank you for your contributions
to help me put together this book for teens.
You are destined for greatness!

To my uncle, Steven Rogers,
thank you for the opportunities
to utilize and expand my business and real estate skills.
You are a blessing!

Acknowledgments

Shawn T. Blanchard - University of Moguls

Sirita Render - S. Render Designs

Keeana Barber - WDB Marketing

Marilyn Alexander - Destined to Publish

TABLE OF CONTENTS

Introduction

I Got the Keys: My Story

I'm rich! I eagerly counted and stuffed all of my money in my pocket and headed to the neighborhood candy store. I was so excited and felt powerful that I could afford to buy a bunch of my favorite sweets. I had the sweetest tooth ever, and nothing was more rewarding then eating a dill pickle with peppermint, penny candy, and flamin' hot chips with nacho cheese, ooh wee. Nobody could tell me nothing. When it was time to pay out, I proudly pulled out all my green hundred-dollar bills to cover the cost. I wanted to impress the owner and show her just how rich I was. But the owner wasn't impressed at all – instead, she appeared to be annoyed and upset that I had asked her to bag up a bunch of sweets, only to present her with fake money from my family's Monopoly real estate board game. She was so angry, with hot cheese already melting through the bag of flamin' hot chips I ordered, and she kicked me out of her store. I remember being so confused, because I honestly thought I was rich, so why was she tripping? To this day, I laugh to myself at that story. But little did I know that my purpose in life was going to be a real-life version of Monopoly in which I would make real money from the real estate industry. I believe that if we pay close attention, God gives us little life clues to guide us to our life's purpose.

After realizing the Monopoly money from the board game was fake, I knew I had to figure out some way to still buy all my sweets. So, I was excited when I was old enough to start working. My first job as a teenager was on the South Side of Chicago in a multi-unit building. I assisted my boss with painting apartments as he got them ready for new tenants to move in. I found painting to be a messy job, as I had to put on clothing only to damage it with paint marks on my clothes, shoes, nails, and even sometimes in my hair and eyelids. But even though I hated the task, I loved to see the finished work. To this day as an adult, I still love the smell and look of a freshly painted room. But what I loved most was getting paid: I earned real money, and at a real young age, from real estate.

My boss was an intelligent, determined, outspoken, handy businessman, who was firm yet giving and gentle inside. My first boss was my dad, John P. Rogers. My dad had my siblings and me help him paint and repair his rental properties to get them ready for new tenants to move in. I am the fifth of my dad's eight children, and as the youngest of his four girls, I was often given the lesser tasks and limited to just painting walls. Sometimes my dad would have one of us stand by and watch him while handing him tools as he would explain how to fix pipes, a furnace, a sink, etc. As a teen, it all went over my head – I was most intrigued with the fact that my dad owned and managed the property. My dad, Mr. Rogers, was the boss and the owner; he was the man. From far off, I watched my dad as the tenants came to him to discuss their issues and paid him money to stay in the building. However, owning and managing real estate was not my father's main job; he was also a supervisor at the Cook County Juvenile Detention Center, where he worked in various capacities. In essence, my dad made additional money from his real estate investments while also working his 9-5 job. While I didn't fully understand everything as a teen, I knew that my dad was the man in charge of the building that we lived in, and it left a lasting impression on me.

As I got older, yet still a teenager, we moved to a house that my parents also owned while still owning the multi-unit building. After graduating from high school and returning from college out of state, I moved into one of my parents' buildings as a tenant. My parents became my first and only landlord until I earned my bachelor's degree. Eventually, my parents decided to sell the building that I resided in, and it was time to finally get out there on my own. While I was terrified, I knew it was time for me to model what I had been exposed to all my life. I wasn't even sure of my career field, yet I was a hundred percent certain that I wanted to invest in real estate. So, I started looking for buildings for almost a year until I brought my first multi-unit property at the age of 22 in the Roseland community on the South Side of Chicago. Finally, what I was shown as a teen became my reality as a young adult: I GOT THE KEYS to own and manage my own property.

Since then, I have purchased more properties, and I even lost it all at one point – life happens. But because I developed an ownership mindset at a young age, I bounced back and was able to start investing in real estate again and on a higher level. Today I am a licensed Managing Real Estate Broker, owner of my own real estate company, R' Legacy Realty, and a property manager for other property owners, all while I continue to invest in real estate for myself.

While my dad introduced me to the real estate industry as a teen, my mom taught me the importance of being educated to help educate others. My mother, Donna Sr., is an educator and worked many years as a schoolteacher for the Chicago Public Schools system. I am also an educator; I work part-time as an Adjunct Business Professor and a licensed Pre-licensing Real Estate Instructor. To this day, I bounce my teaching lessons and speaking engagements off my mother for her feedback, since she instilled in me the gift of teaching. As such, I have created multiple streams of income as a business and real estate educator as well.

I am blessed to have been exposed to real estate as a teen. However, I realized that not everyone is afforded that opportunity of exposure at a young age. This is especially true within the black community, where the rate of black homeownership is lower than any other ethnicity. Moreover, wealth can be created through homeownership; as such, blacks have the lowest rate of wealth in in the US as well. Therefore, it is imperative to intentionally empower the black community to become homeowners, and it starts with youth.

Who got the keys? For me, my parents had the keys, and they gave me the keys of information that empowered me to go get the actual keys of homeownership for myself, which is much more impactful and lasting. Now that I have my keys, it is important to help the next generation to do the same. My purpose in life and for this book is to do what my parents did for me: expose and equip today's black teens to become tomorrow's homeowners and investors. So, let's get started.

Welcome, class, to *Building Generational Wealth Through Real Estate!* As a student in this class, your participation and feedback is required. Throughout this course, I will be asking you, "WHO GOT THE KEYS?" Whenever you have gained new keys of information from reading this book, I need you to declare, "I GOT THE KEYS!" because your words can manifest into your realty.

By the end of this course, you will be exposed, empowered, and equipped to obtain and maintain real estate that can be passed down generationally.

MY JOURNEY TO SECURING THE KEYS TO REAL ESTATE

EXPOSED
As a teen, my 1st job was at my parents' building

ELEVATED
As a young adult, I purchased my 1st multi-unit property

EMPOWERED
My parents passed the keys to homeownership to me

Sold by

R' Legacy Realty
www.rlegacyrealty.com
(312)-276-5111

NEW HOMEOWNER
I Got the Keys!
Building Generational Wealth

Rogers Family

CHAPTER ONE

KEEPING IT REAL ABOUT REAL ESTATE

The Basics of Real Estate and Building Wealth

CHAPTER

1

Knock, knock, knock... knock, knock... knock, knock! Have you ever been locked outside of your house, while constantly knocking on the door and eagerly waiting for someone to open it for you? You just got home from class, work, or hanging out, and now you are ready to just chill in the house. However, no one is coming to the door. It can be quite annoying to wait for someone to open a door to give you access to the home, especially if it's cold and/ or raining outside. Delayed access. I remember those moments of frustration, rushing home to my favorite TV show or snack only for someone inside the house to take longer than expected to open the door for me. But what I remember more is the day that my parents felt I was mature enough not to have to deal with those moments of delayed access anymore, because I finally received my own key!

I no longer had to wait for the door to be opened for me, because I was empowered to let myself in with my own key. Whether referring to the little metal object you put in the lock to turn it, or to valuable information or a solution, the purpose of a key remains the same: keys give access. As you become a student of the real estate industry, you will receive some powerful keys of information and solutions in hopes of leading you to obtain physical keys to real estate that you own.

So, what is real estate? Where you currently live is real estate; the school building you attend is real estate; the place where you go to shop, eat, watch movies, or hang out at is real estate. Technically, real estate is the land and everything built on it – the improvements. This includes the ground you walk on, the air space above us, and the subsurface of what is under the land, in addition to the public and private places that are man-made onto it (*Modern Real Estate Practice in Illinois*, 10th edition Dearborn Real Estate Education). It's also important to know that there are different types of real estate that are used for different purposes, including residential, commercial, agricultural, industrial, and special use real estate. Let's look at each type of real estate and review examples in Figure 1.

» **Residential real estate** generally refers to property meant for people to reside or live in, whether it is a house, apartment, condo, or permanently attached mobile home.

» **Commercial real estate** is property used for business. Examples of commercial real estate are gyms, clothing stores, movie theaters, hotels, office spaces, and even parking lots.

» **Agricultural real estate** deals with land used to produce crops and raise livestock. Examples include ranches, orchards, and farms.

» **Industrial real estate** is used to manufacture products. Warehouses and factories are examples of industrial real estate.

» **Special purpose real estate** is real estate designed for a particular purpose, such as schools, churches, parks, cemeteries, and government-owned land.

Every type of real estate has an owner, whether it is an individual, family, business, organization, or government entity. Property owners have the right to possess, control, enjoy, exclude, and dispose of their property (*Modern Real Estate Practice in Illinois*, 10th edition, Dearborn Real Estate Education). As such, property owners may buy,

EXAMPLES OF
REAL ESTATE TYPES
(Figure 1)

RESIDENTIAL

COMMERCIAL

AGRICULTURAL

INDUSTRIAL

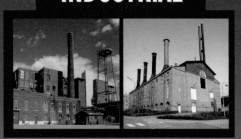

SPECIAL PURPOSE

rent out, and/or sell real estate to their own benefit. The benefits of property ownership include a sense of pride and the freedom to enjoy the property with fewer restrictions than a renter, but the greatest benefit is the potential financial gain from owning real estate.

Real estate is an asset; in essence, it is something of value. Therefore, owning real estate can add financial value to your life. But these property rights and benefits are not all available to people who chose to rent property as opposed to owning it. To rent a property means you have to pay someone else to live or operate a business or/and activity on their property temporarily. On the other hand, owners pay a mortgage. A mortgage is a monthly payment to pay back the cost you owe to buy the property. As you pay down your mortgage, you build up your equity, which is when you owe less on a property than it is worth. So, whether a person decides to just own the home they live in or several properties, in general, owners tend to have a higher financial status (net worth) than a person who rents. Homeowners' median net worth is 40 times that of renters, according to the Federal Reserves.

While owning property will require more responsibility, the financial gain and opportunity to build wealth makes ownership in real estate highly worth investing in. As owners continue to acquire more assets of real estate, they can continue to increase their income and accumulate wealth generationally.

Wealth Building

Imagine being able to buy your favorite clothing, shoes, phone, jewelry, or car and still have more than enough money left over. Being wealthy will allow you the ability to do just that. According to Webster's Dictionary, wealth is "an abundance of valuable possessions or money; the state of being rich; material prosperity; or a plentiful supply of a particular desirable thing." To me, wealth is the abundance of money, good health, and peace of mind. Besides, what good is it to have a lot of money if you cannot enjoy it, right? But for the sake of this book, we will focus on financial wealth generated through real estate, as multimillionaire Andrew Carnegie said that "ninety percent of all millionaires do so through real estate." With the right skills sets and characteristics you can make an abundance of money through real estate investing also.

For you to earn an abundance of money through real estate, you have to be willing to work hard and properly prepare. Even at your age, you can prepare yourself by becoming a student of the industry now and learning more about topics on financial literacy, business, and real estate. Learning how to be financially disciplined and taking care of your financial needs before your wants will help you to maintain the property as well. The more aware you are about real estate, the more prepared you become to make well-informed decisions, and the better you position yourself to start investing at an early age. Buying property at a younger age helps to build up more wealth at an older age. The earlier you buy property, the sooner you will be able to pay it off, have less debt, and become more financially secure.

As you become financially successful, you will be able to enjoy more of your wants after you take care of your financial needs. Whether you find enjoyment in buying the latest fashion or car, engaging in your favorite hobby, traveling, or chilling with friends, remember as

DID YOU KNOW?

"

Buying property at a younger age helps to build up more wealth at an older age.

"

you build your wealth to first pay debts off, save money, and also give back to others. *"It is more blessed to give than to receive"* (Acts 20:35, KJV). Once you have the keys to unlock doors to build wealth though real estate, be the key to help your peers and the younger people around you to do the same. As it is important to obtain real estate to build wealth, it is just as important to maintain it from generation to generation.

If you got some keys from this chapter, declare it, "I got the keys!"

CHAPTER TWO

BLACK HOMEOWNERSHIP MATTERS

Real Estate and Racism

CHAPTER

2

Now imagine, you're continuously knocking on the door, and you are certain that the people inside can hear you knocking, and they can even see you through the peephole. Yet they choose to ignore you and refuse to open the door, denying you access to the inside, simply because of the color of your skin! In real life, housing discrimination and segregation denied blacks access and rights to rent, own, and sell real estate for many years. Moreover, homeownership is a key factor in building wealth, especially within the black community, where nearly sixty percent of wealth for black homeowners comes from home equity (when the property value is higher than the amount you owe on it) (Urban Institute, 2020 Closing the Gaps: Building Black Wealth through Homeownership Report). But to economically oppress the black community from building wealth, governmental offices, often led by whites, put discriminatory rules and regulations in place to prevent or delay black families from claiming their right to own real estate, which negatively impacted their ability to create or accumulate more wealth.

40 Acres & a Mule

In 1863, slavery was abolished after 244 years of blacks being abused and working for free as contractors, builders, farmers, and property managers of real estate for their white slave owners. In January of 1865, General William T. Sherman and others met with black ministers and leaders to ask: "What do you want for your own people" following the civil war? The response was, "Land!" ("The Truth Behind 40 Acres and a Mule," www.pbs.org). Even back then, blacks wanted redistribution of land ownership, because they understood the financial benefits and power of owning real estate. As a result of that meeting, Special Field Order 15 was created and approved by President Abraham Lincoln in an effort to financially compensate blacks for the years of abuse and free labor on plantations. The order, known as "40 Acres and a Mule," would allow former slaves to each own up to 40 acres of land and a mule (also known as a donkey), which farmers use for transportation and to carry supplies. But later that year, when Andrew Johnson became president after Lincoln's assassination, the order was reversed and denied ("The Truth Behind 40 Acres and a Mule," www.pbs.org). In essence, government officials stood at the door of property ownership as blacks knocked and waited for access to their rights for equal housing and reparations, but they were denied once again to prevent the economic and financial empowerment of the black community.

Moreover, blacks continued to be treated as second-class citizens and could not live in certain neighborhoods that were more resourceful and better established, which tended to be predominantly white areas. Often when a black family tried to live in a more upscale community that they could afford to live in, they were still rejected or even forced out after being harassed. If that didn't work, then a majority of the white neighbors would relocate for fear that the property values would decrease due to the presence of a black family. This is known as blockbusting. While some white families blockbusted out of the community due to black families moving in, other whites were steered away from moving into communities where a black family resided for the same reason.

Homeownership is said to be the American dream, yet for many black Americans, there tends to be a lack of financial resources made accessible for it to become a reality. Most people take out a loan, known as a mortgage, to buy property. To qualify for the mortgage, a person must meet certain financial standards (discussed in detail in Chapter 3) for the lender to release the money to buy a property. However, blacks were often denied access to loan money to purchase real estate or charged higher fees despite being financially qualified to afford the loan, because of the color of their skin.

Redlining

In 1934, the federal government created the Federal Housing Administration (FHA) to restore the housing market after the Great Depression as the economy as a whole suffered. New governmental systems and programs were created such as the New Deal and the Home Owners' Loan Corporation (HOLC). The New Deal provided incentives and financial assistance to help people to become new homeowners, while the HOLC helped current homeowners to refinance (redo the loan for better rates). their current mortgage loan. But this government assistance to help encourage and maintain homeownership did not apply to everyone. Instead, racist restrictions were put in place that allowed banks and other financial institutions to deny, delay, or charge black people higher fees for mortgage loans. In essence, the federal government created systems and programs that allowed banks and other financial institutions to implement redlining. Redlining is when lenders discriminate on loan applications by refusing to lend to someone or charging higher rates and fees based on the person's race or ethnicity, or within certain communities. These communities were predominantly black or brown, and a color-coded map was created with red lines drawn around them to indicate that the community was hazardous. This color-coded map was used by lenders to indicate the race or financial class that predominantly resided in a particular community. For example:

» Green: The best communities in high demand, where professional white people lived.

» Blue: Still desirable and stable communities where whites lived.

» Yellow: Definitely declining communities that bordered black communities and were at risk of foreign-born, negro, or "low-grade" populations moving in.

» Red: Hazardous communities where the majority of the black and brown people lived, regardless of their financial status.

("The History of Redlining," www.thoughtco.com)

Everyone should have the right to obtain a loan to buy property that is solely based on their ability to meet certain financial qualifications and standards, not their race. However, lenders were allowed to reject, delay, or charge higher lending fees to loan applicants who lived in communities with red lines around them, as well as some yellow lines. Redlining is a form of systemic racism that has significantly lowered the rate of homeownership amongst the black community. In 2020, the rate of black homeownership and wealth is still the lowest amongst all races in the US, while whites have the highest rate of homeownership and wealth (see infographic: Who Got the Keys in the US?). Though redlining is illegal now, research shows that black Americans still tend to pay higher fees and rates for mortgage loans and are more likely to be denied loans to buy real estate than other applicants (NAREB, 2020 State of Housing in Black America Report). This systemic racism continues to economically oppress the black community because it creates barriers to a key factor to building black wealth, which is homeownership. This is why black homeownership matters!

The impact of years of racial inequality and housing segregation is still reflected in many major cities today. For example, in Chicago, the majority of blacks live on the south, east, and a portion of the west side of the city, while the majority of whites live up north, downtown,

Who Got the Keys in the US?

Homeownership is a key to build wealth. Yet Blacks have the lowest rate of homeownership and wealth.

Rate of Homeownership by Race

BLACKS 44.1%　　**WHITES** 74.5%　　**HISPANICS** 49.1%　　**OTHER RACES** 56.3%

— *US Census Bureau 2020*

Rate of Homeownership Before Age 35 by Race

BLACKS 10.8%　　**WHITES** 35%　　**HISPANICS** 22.7%　　**ASIAN** 24.1%

— *NAREB, 2020 State of Housing in Black America Report*

Median Net Worth Per Race

(what you *own* minus what you *owe*)

BLACKS $24,100　　**WHITES** $188,200　　**HISPANICS** $36,100　　**OTHER RACES** $74,500

— *Federal Reserves, 2019 Survey of Consumer Finances*

and in portions of the west side where property values are higher and there is more accessibility to the necessities to live comfortably. This is the opposite of the predominantly black neighborhoods that are plagued with boarded-up homes and have limited access to healthy grocery stores, healthcare facilities, and high-performing schools. When there is lower quality or limited access to resources in predominantly black communities, it negatively affects their ability to build wealth at the same rate and level as other communities.

Real Estate Professionals & Race

The real estate profession can be very profitable. The income of a real estate agent or broker (title may vary by state) is based on the value and amount of the properties that the agent helps others to buy, sell, or rent. "Location, location, location" is the main key in determining the value of a property. That means that if you take the same exact property and move it to a different community, the value will be different based on its location. As such, real estate located in mostly black communities tends to have lower values than properties located in mostly white communities ("Redlining Legacy of Inequity: $212,000 Less Home Equity, Low Homeownership Rates for Black Families," www.redfin.com/news). The difference in property values in predominantly white communities versus black communities has a direct and negative effect on the level of wealth for black homeowners. Moreover, it affects the level of income for black real estate agents as well. While the US Census Bureau reports that less than six percent of active real estate agents are black, people tend to hire a real estate agent who looks like them in regard to race and ethnicity. Therefore, a black real estate agent is more likely to get hired by a black person looking to buy, sell, or lease a property within a predominately black community that has lower property values. As a result, black real estate agents are often forced to close on even more deals or try to work in predominantly white communities to increase the amount of income they can generate from property sales.

Keys to Progress & Solutions

Through consistent advocacy and activism, progress has been made to create equal housing opportunities for all people. The Civil Rights Act of 1964 prohibited discrimination based on race or color in government-assisted housing programs. Four years later, Title VIII of the Civil Rights Act of 1968, known as the Fair Housing Act, made it illegal for anyone to discriminate in housing based on race, color, religion, or national origin. As such, real estate professionals and lenders can lose their license and be penalized if they are found guilty of discriminating. Additionally, economic empowerment groups such as the National Association for the Advancement of Colored People (NAACP) and the National Association of Real Estate Brokers (NAREB) were established many years ago to advocate for equal rights, resources, and economic empowerment for the black community, which includes increasing the rate of black homeownership. Nevertheless, the rate of black homeownership and wealth remains the lowest amongst all other races in the US. Therefore, it is imperative for the government to be intentional about encouraging black homeownership by creating programs and resources similar to what they made in the past, which were most beneficial to whites, to end the great economic depression that continues to plague the black community.

As a young person, it is important for you to know that black homeownership does matter and to understand the past and current state of black homeownership. It is also important for black youth to be more exposed and educated about homeownership as a key to build wealth, to help increase their likelihood of becoming homeowners or investors in the future and at an earlier age. The infographic, Who Got the Keys in the US? shows that blacks are less likely to become homeowners by age 35 than any other race. The earlier you buy real estate, the sooner you can pay off the debt you owe on the property, if any, which gives you more equity. Remember, real estate adds value, it's an asset, so greater equity in a property yields a higher financial status. Everyone deserves equal ability to accumulate wealth through homeownership at the same rate and level. Therefore, we must be intentional to ensure that all people have equal rights and access to housing and resources to live, buy, sell, or rent real estate in whatever area they can afford. This book represents my intention to do so by empowering today's teens to build wealth by becoming tomorrow's homeowners and investors.

Future homeowner, who got the keys?

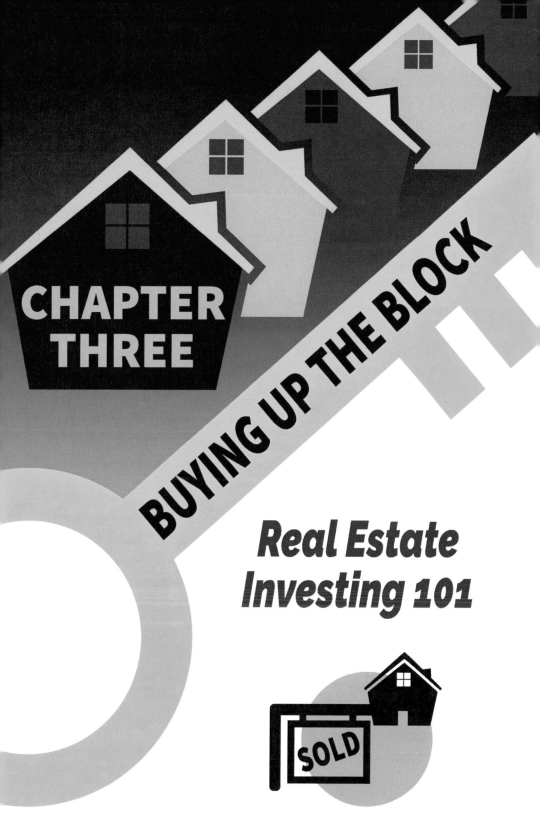

CHAPTER THREE

BUYING UP THE BLOCK

Real Estate Investing 101

SOLD

CHAPTER

3

Just like the real estate board game of Monopoly, the goal of a real estate investor is to buy up as much profitable real estate as possible to build up their portfolio of wealth. Remember ninety percent of all millionaires do so through real estate, according to multimillionaire Andrew Carnegie. To effectively implement this goal, it is imperative to identify the purpose of the property type you want to buy, know how to acquire the property, and understand the home buying process, while preparing the funding to buy a property. Proper preparation to buy real estate will help you to be more successful in meeting your real estate goals. Let's look at the keys of preparation for success.

Real Estate Exit Strategies

There are various ways to invest and make lots of money from real estate. What works for one person may be different for another, yet they both can be equally successful. Therefore, it's important to be aware of the various exit strategies and opportunities for you to decide your plan of execution. A real estate exit strategy is based on your purpose for investing in the property and what you intend to do with the property once you acquire it. There are several exit strategies for real estate as follows:

Wholesaling

A wholesaler finds property owners who are willing to sell their homes for less than what their properties are worth. Then the wholesaler signs a purchasing contract with the homeowner. Next, the wholesaler finds an investor who is willing and able to buy that same property "as-is" (in its current condition and without additional repairs being made) for cash right away but for a higher price. Many times, the sale date between the wholesaler and the owner takes place on the same date as the sale between the wholesaler and the investor for the purchase of the property. Ultimately, the wholesaler gets to keep the difference between the amount the investor paid for the property minus the amount the owner agreed to sell their home for. The key is to buy low and sell high.

For example: Mia's exit strategy is to wholesale real estate. As such, she has a purchasing contract with Amari to buy his home for $50,000. Then Mia gets Cory, an investor, to agree to buy this same property as-is for $67,000 in cash. One the same day that she buys Amari's house, Cory immediately buys it from her. As a result, Mia profited $17,000 from the two transactions.

Fix & Flip

Investors find a property, fund it, fix it, and then flip it for a higher price. The key is to find a property that the investor can buy and rehab because the after-repair value (ARV) will be higher. In essence, the total cost to buy and repair the property is less than the price to sell it. Additionally, investors must be mindful of the expenses they have to pay to hold the property until it is sold; this is called holding cost. Examples of holding costs are utilities, lawn care, mortgage payments, and other fees. Lastly, investors must also calculate the closing cost, which is the cost to buy and sell real estate. Examples of closing costs may include attorney fees, transfer stamp fees, lender fees, realtor fees, and more. Closing costs apply to all real estate sales transactions; however, the amount per transaction and who pays may vary.

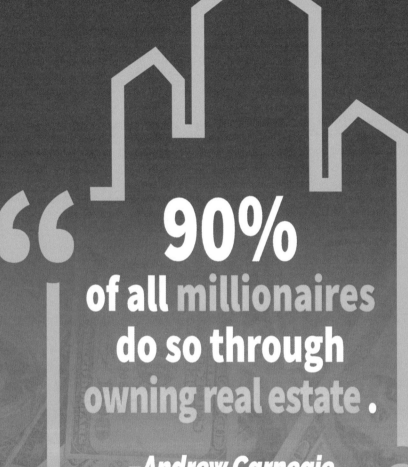

DID YOU KNOW?

" **90%**
of all millionaires
do so through
owning real estate .

-Andrew Carnegie

"

For example: Angel is an investor whose exit strategy is to fix and flip real estate, so she finds the following property to invest in:

$60,000 – Purchasing price

$40,000 – Amount paid to rehab

$7,000 – Holding cost

$6,000 – Closing cost

$113,000 – Total cost of all these expenses together

Four months later, Angel sells the same house at the after-repair value of $180,000. Angel makes a profit of $67,000 ($180,000 ARV - $113,000 total cost) from her fix and flip investment.

Buy & Hold

Investors buy an income-producing property and hold it to rent it out to others. If the investor/owner chooses to occupy a unit in their property, the key is to buy a property that will at least cover its monthly expenses as much as possible from the income the property generates. However, if the investor/owner will not live on the property, then the key is for the rent to cover the monthly expenses and produce a profit. When deciding to buy and hold real estate, an investor should do a property analysis to determine how much income and profit the property will generate on a monthly and annual basis. Below are the amounts and formulas to complete a basic property analysis:

Revenue/Income: The total amount of money that the property generates each month (or year). This may include rent, parking fees, washer/dryer machines, and/or vending machines.

Key: Sometimes you may make less money in a particular month because tenants may miss a payment or because you have a percentage of vacant units waiting to be rented out, which is called the vacancy rate.

Expenses: The cost to operate and maintain the property, such as utilities, lawn care, snow removal, cleaning, repairs, advertisement, property taxes, insurance, property management costs, etc. (Important note: this does not include the principal nor interest of mortgage payments).

Net Operating Income (NOI): Revenue/income minus expenses. The goal is to ensure that the total income is higher than the total expenses.

Cash Flow: NOI minus the debt service. Debt service is the amount required to repay the principal (amount of the loan) and interest (fee to borrow money) on a loan (debt) for a certain timeframe.

The key is to have a high cash flow from your investment property.

For example: VJ is an investor who wants to buy and hold a two-unit property. VJ will take out a loan to buy the property with an annual debt service of $6,900. As such, he runs an analysis on the property as follows:

$24,000 - Total annual revenue/income

$4,800 - Total annual operating expenses

$19,200 - Net operating income ($24,000 income - $4,800 expenses)

$12,300 - Cash flow ($19,200 NOI - $6,900 annual debt service amount)

From this two-unit building, VJ would profit $12,300 a year. If VJ holds this property for 30 years, he may make $369,000 in total. Additionally, if VJ pays off the full principal and interest due in 30 years, his annual cash flow would significantly increase.

Key: You can sell a rental property at any time; just ensure there are no rules from your lender to keep the property for a certain number of years before you can sell it.

Seller Financing: The owner/investor will allow a buyer to pay them monthly payments to purchase their property, as opposed to the buyer taking out a loan with a bank or lending institution. In essence, the seller acts as the lender. In the event the buyer stops making payments or violates the contract terms, the seller can take the property back. It's important to utilize a real estate attorney to help negotiate and write up a detail contract between the owner and the buyer.

For example: Jakkia's exit strategy is to sell her property and serve as the lender to qualified buyer, Nature. As such, she negotiates the sales price of her property and the monthly payments for Nature to cover the loan amount, insurance, property taxes, plus interest. In the event Nature is late making a payment, she must pay a late fee. If Nature stops making payments, Jakkia can take the house back and keep any payments made previously.

Income Types

There are different types of income that you can make from investing in real estate, depending on your exit strategy:

> » **Active** – Income earned from short-term investments such as wholesaling and fix and flips.

» **Passive** – Income earned from long-term investments such as buy and holds.

You can also make money from real estate investing by earning interest, which is the cost people pay to use other people's money.

» **Interest** – Income earned from the cost of others using your money, such as lending money to other real estate investors or paying others tax liens (details provided in the next section).

Now that you know the different types of income you can earn from real estate and your exit strategy, you will need to decide how to acquire real estate.

Different Ways to Acquire Real Estate -

When you become the owner of real estate, you will receive a deed. A deed is the document that identifies ownership of a particular property. Below are some ways you can acquire a property to receive the deed.

Tax Liens: All property owners must pay their property taxes (charged by the county that the property is located in). However, owners may fall behind on paying their taxes, accumulating fees and interest. As such, the county in which the property is located will facilitate tax sales throughout the year to get the past due property tax debt paid off. The public can bid on the property at the tax sales (be sure the property is worth the amount you bid). If you win the bid and pay off the past due taxes on someone else's property at the tax sales, there are two options:

1. The owner gets a redemption period, which is the time period given to the owner to buy the taxes back; this time period varies per state. To redeem the property, the owner must pay back the full amount of the past due taxes, including the late

fees and interest due. The person who originally paid the past due taxes will receive their money back *plus* extra money from the interest that was charged while the owners waited to buy the taxes back.

2. If the owner does not pay the past due taxes by the end of the redemption period, you will get the tax deed on the property and become the new owner. The process to get the ownership transferred over through a tax deed may vary per state. There are professionals who charge fees to locate the best properties to buy the past due taxes for. You should also use a real estate attorney with experience in tax liens to assist in the deed transfer.

Real Estate Investment Trust (REIT): You can invest in a company that buys and manages income-producing real estate and allows others to invest (shareholders) in the company without having to buy and manage the property themselves. Shareholders (the investors) receive a portion of the profits from the diverse portfolio of real estate owned, operated and/or financed by the REIT. It is important to research and fully understand all of the stipulations for membership and payouts.

Lease Options (Rent to Own): You can rent a property until you are able to buy it. You will have two agreements, the first being a lease agreement, where the owner will charge you a monthly amount to rent the property. Then the second agreement will be a purchase agreement, where a portion of your monthly payment goes toward the amount the owner is selling the property for. At some point, the goal is for you to get enough money to pay off the balance on the amount owed to fully purchase the property and stop renting it. I recommend you have a real estate attorney to review the agreement on your behalf before you commit to the terms and conditions.

Traditional Home Purchasing: Many people buy a property from an owner outright by paying all cash or taking out a loan from a bank or lending institution. The owner, also known as the seller, puts their property up for sale in hopes that someone will purchase it for the highest price possible. However, the goal for a buyer is to purchase a property for the lowest reasonable price. The buyer and/or seller may use a real estate agent to help them buy or sell the property because agents are very knowledgeable about the real estate market, help negotiate deals more effectively, and help to solve problems that may occur during the home buying process. After a series of events (see flowchart: 12 Steps to Securing the Keys), the lender pays the seller the full purchasing price as agreed, the deed is transferred to the buyer as the new owner, and then the buyer begins to make monthly payments to their lender (if they didn't pay cash) to pay off the loan. Regardless of the process, which may vary by state, buyers must be financially prepared and stable to purchase real estate.

Where to Get Money to Buy Real Estate

In order to buy real estate, you will need to get a pre-approval for a mortgage loan, unless you have access to a lot of cash. The monthly mortgage payment may include the principal (amount of the loan), property insurance (coverage for damage or loss), property taxes (charged by the county that the property is located in), and interest (cost to borrow money), this is called the PITI. The type of loan and lender to seek a pre-approval from is based on the exit strategy and property type. For example, if you want to fix and flip a property, you should look for a lender that will lend you money to buy and rehab the property, then sell it as soon as possible. Each lender has their own processes and qualifications to get a mortgage loan from them. Nevertheless, all lenders tend to look at the 5 C's of credit to assess your financial status: capital, capacity, collateral, credit, and character. Let's examine each in detail:

Capital: You must have some cash in your bank account(s) to qualify to buy property. Lenders will look for savings accounts and others assets that you may have to afford the loan. Even with a loan, it is important for you to have savings to demonstrate you are financially disciplined and have the ability to make a down payment and cover closing costs. Lenders will require you to have a portion of the money to put down towards the purchasing price before they will lend you the remaining amount owed to the seller/owner.

Capacity: Lenders will assess your ability to repay the loan by asking for the various sources of consistent income that you receive and stable employment. Lenders will require documentation to prove each source of income. They will also calculate your total monthly income in comparison to your total monthly household expenses (such as rent or mortgage payments) and non-household expenses (such as student and auto loans), known as your debt service ratios.

Collateral: Lenders assess the type, condition, and location of the actual property you want to buy to make certain it is a good investment. Lenders may also assess how profitable the investment property is in addition to its value. A property must be appraised to ensure that the property value is equal or greater to the cost you are paying for the property.

Credit: Everyone is given a credit score, ranging from 0 to 800, to rate their creditworthiness. Creditworthiness indicates how worthy you are to receive products or services before paying for them. The higher your credit score, the easier it will be to get loans for lower interest rates and fees to buy real estate or other products. Your credit score is developed over time and is based on the following five factors:

1. Credit Utilization – the amount of debt owed

2. Credit History – how long the debt is owed

3. Credit Mix – the different types of credit accounts opened

4. New Credit – the number of new credit accounts opened and inquiries from credit applications to companies

5. Payment History – how often you make payments on time (the most important factor in determining your credit score)

Character: This is also one of the five C's of credit. It is an assessment of your integrity with regard to the management of your finances. The lender looks at all the factors together, including your employment history, the amount of debt you have, and your credit score, to tell a story about the likelihood that you can and will repay the mortgage loan on time.

The lender will either pre-approve you for a mortgage loan or inform you of the steps to take to qualify in the future. Once you are pre-approved, the lender will tell you the loan type, the amount you qualify for, and an estimate of the down payment amount and closing costs to buy the property.

KEY: Always research and ask a lender if they know of any grants or down payment assistance programs that you may qualify for to help you cover the expenses to buy a property. Be sure to know all of the stipulations of any grants and down payment assistance programs beforehand.

Whether you have access to cash or need to take out a mortgage loan to buy real estate, it's important to maintain stable employment, pay your bills on time, have a savings account, and continue to build up your credit score. The more financially stable you are, the more properties you will be able to purchase to build wealth and enjoy life.

12 Steps to Secure the Keys to Homeownership

Now that you have your exit strategy and the funding to purchase real estate, you are ready to start shopping for your new property. Let's review the steps to the home buying process, which may vary slightly by state.

See Flowchart- 12 Steps to Secure the Keys

1. Interview and consult with a real estate agent to discuss your real estate goals and needs and how the agent can best serve you. My office, R' Legacy Realty, has a team of agents that provide equal residential and commercial housing opportunities and services, check out www.rlegacyrealty.com.

2. Based on the property type, size, location(s), condition, and other must-have details provided by you, the real estate agent will send you property listings to look through. Afterwards, you will notify your agent of the properties that you want to view in person to schedule a showing.

3. Once you find the right property, you will let your agent know that you are willing, ready, and able to purchase it by submitting an offer.

4. Before submitting your offer, have the real estate agent complete a comparative analysis for you, also known as a market analysis, to determine the amount you want to offer the seller. A comp analysis compares and tells you what the current prices are for similarly situated properties within the same location. You want to ensure that the asking price for the property that you want to buy is close to or less than the prices of similar properties in that area. You also want a market analysis to determine the after-repair value (ARV) of a property that you want to fix and flip, to ensure it is profitable.

5. Once you have decided on the price that you want to offer the seller, you will sign a purchasing contract, and your agent will submit your offer to the seller or their real estate agent. Once your offer is submitted, the negotiation process begins. The time frame may vary, so patience is the key in negotiations.

At this point, the seller may accept, reject, or counter (respond with a different amount or terms for you to decide on) your offer. If rejected, you have to start back at step 2 to continue house shopping. But if you reach an agreement and your offer is accepted, you can proceed with the process.

6. Once the seller and buyer complete and sign the purchasing contract, the deal is official. Copies should be sent to the other real estate professionals on your team, such as your real estate attorney and/or lender, to start processing the transaction.

7. Buyers must submit earnest money for their accepted offer, which is good faith money to the seller to demonstrate that the buyer is serious about buying the property. The amount may vary. This money is held in a special account and is credited back to the buyer at the closing (when ownership is transferred from the seller to the buyer). However, if the deal is canceled, the earnest money may be refunded back to the buyer, unless the seller challenges the refund.

8. The buyer hires a home inspector or general contractor (GC) to identify any issues with the property. For example, they will test and assess the electrical, roofing, plumbing, heating, and cooling systems to ensure they operate properly. A buyer may request that the seller make certain repairs before they purchase the home. But if a property is sold "as is," the seller will not make any repairs. In this case, the buyer's contractors will help to calculate the cost of all repairs to determine if the property is still worth investing in.

9. An appraiser is sent to the property to determine if the property is worth less than, equal to, or more than the purchasing price that the seller and buyer agreed to. Depending on the funding source, the lender or buyer may order and send out the appraiser.

   Key: The lender will not release the loan money if the property does not appraise for the purchasing amount that buyer and seller agreed to or less. While the seller is not obligated to, the seller can agree to lower the purchasing price to the appraised valued to move forward with the transaction.

10. A title search is conducted to ensure that the title (ownership rights) on the property is clear and that there are no barriers that would prevent the owner from selling the property to the buyer. For example, if an owner has past due taxes, a tax lien may be placed on the property. Tax liens must be paid in full before a property can be sold.

11. Once the lender has completed a thorough analysis of the buyer's ability to afford and pay back the mortgage loan, the lender will release a clearance to close. Then the closing date is scheduled for ownership to transfer from the seller to the buyer.

12. The buyer, along with their real estate agent, takes a final walk-through of the property to ensure that the seller completed all requested repairs as agreed, if any. Also, the final walk-through is to make sure that the property is in the same or better condition than it was at the time of the buyer's previous walk-through of the property.

Now it's time to close on this real estate transaction and get your keys to your new property!

12 STEPS TO SECURE THE KEYS

Process after securing funding

01 CONSULT WITH YOUR REAL ESTATE AGENT R' Legacy Realty

02 GET PROPERTY LISTINGS & START HOUSE SHOPPING

03 CHOOSE A PROPERTY TO PUT AN OFFER ON TO BUY

04 GET A COMPARATIVE aka MARKET ANALYSIS

05 SUBMIT OFFER TO SELLER *If rejected, back to step 2*

06 SEND COPIES OF THE SIGNED CONTRACT TO YOUR TEAM

07 SUBMIT EARNEST MONEY

08 CONDUCT A HOME INSPECTION

09 APPRAISER DETERMINES THE PROPERTY VALUE

10 A TITLE SEARCH IS CONDUCTED

11 TRANSACTION IS CLEARED TO CLOSE

12 COMPLETE A FINAL WALK THROUGH AT THE PROPERTY

GET YOUR KEYS AT CLOSING!

Sold by
R' Legacy Realty
www.rlegacyrealty.com
(312)-276-5111

NEW HOMEOWNER
I Got the Keys!
Building Generational Wealth

Process may vary by state

Investors may decide to diversify their exit strategies and property types as they continue to buy property. Nevertheless, whether you buy one or many properties on the block, buying real estate is empowering and a major life accomplishment. It is also a major achievement for teenagers to learn these keys of homeownership early to help avoid financial pitfalls and to get a head start on building wealth through real estate. So, even as a teen, I challenge you to use these keys of information to think like a boss by mentally preparing to secure the actual keys to property that you will own in the future.

Future investor, declare out loud, "I got the keys!"

CHAPTER FOUR

ACT LIKE A TEEN BUT THINK LIKE A BOSS
Managing Real Estate

A boss is someone who's in charge. Even as a teen, you are a boss because you are in charge of your words, thoughts, and actions, demonstrating good character. The better you can manage yourself, the more successful you will be in effectively managing real estate for yourself and others in the future. But being just a boss is not enough – a boss who makes a positive impact on the lives of others is next level.

Let's look at qualities of next-level bosses:

» Appreciate their own uniqueness and stay true to their purpose and life journey

» Do not need validation from others to determine their value

» Have integrity because their words and actions are the same

» Inspire and encourage others to do and be their best

» Do not deceive or tear others down to make themselves feel better or to get ahead

» Acknowledge their feelings but don't allow their feelings to impulsively dictate their actions

» Communicate effectively, which includes listening to others

» Are not perfect, but they take responsibility and accountability for their actions

» Are reliable and dependable, honoring other people's time

» Care about the well-being of others, while maintaining healthy self-care

» Self-reflect on their strengths and areas of improvement and take the necessary steps to be the best version of themselves through the various stages of life

Having a positive character can attract the right people and the right opportunities for you to reach and maintain success. I heard a powerful pastor named Bishop T.D. Jakes once preach, "Your gift can take you places that your character won't keep you." In essence, we all have natural talents and gifts that will guide us to our purpose in life and open doors of opportunities, but we may fail and lose those opportunities if we have bad character or an attitude. This is especially important as a real estate professional because the industry is very people driven, and people like to work with and hire professionals who are skillful and have a positive attitude and good character as well.

In addition to positive character, you do need basic skill sets to be successful within the real estate industry. Let's unlock the key skill sets of a next-level boss in real estate, which are also useful in all career fields. The most common and minimum skill sets are as follows:

» **Customer service skills:** In real estate, you will encounter a lot of people with diverse cultures, backgrounds, and needs. Therefore, you must be flexible, respectful, and knowledgeable, while keeping the customer's needs a priority. Excellent customer service aims to exceed your customer's expectations before, during, and after a transaction. How you treat and service others will affect your reputation. Your reputation is a key factor in whether people will continue working with you, recommend and refer you for more opportunities, or deter others from working with you to avoid another bad experience.

» **Organizational skills:** In real estate, you will have to manage appointments and paperwork while meeting deadlines. You will need to maintain a scheduling and filing system to operate efficiently.

» **Communication skills:** In real estate, you will need to be open and able to discuss your products, services, and the industry, as well as listen to your customers' and team members' needs and feedback. It is also important that you always communicate with them in a professional and timely fashion.

» **Team player skills:** Real estate is a team sport in which you will have to work with other professionals to effectively run the business and service your clients. Therefore, you must be people friendly and respect all team members' roles, while contributing your part to complete the end goal.

» **Critical thinking skills:** Real estate professionals will have to deal with issues from tenants, contractors, customers, and others, as anything can come up at any time. As a boss, you must have the ability to quickly think of the most effective way to solve problems, which is why it is important to be well educated about the industry to know updated regulations, strategies, and the processes allowed to solve them.

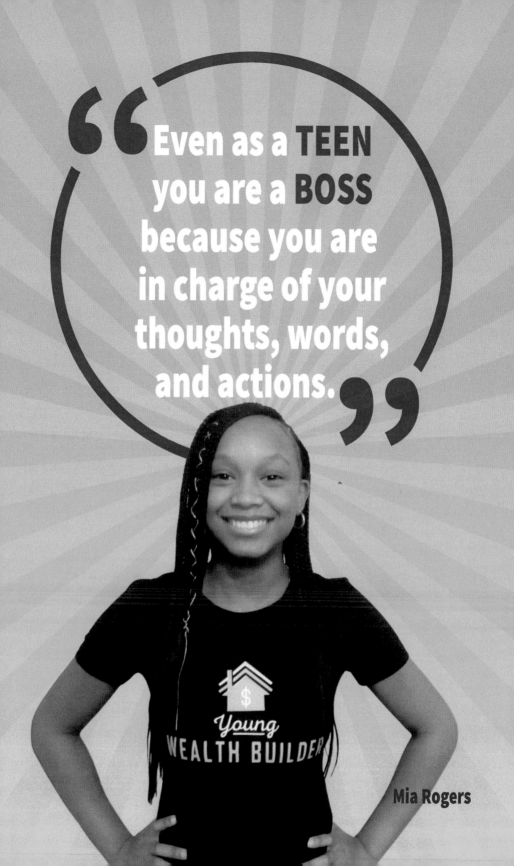

» **Computer skills:** We live in a technology-driven society now, and the real estate industry is always using new apps and online systems to stay current and make processes smoother. You must have basic computer skills; be active on social media; and stay updated on new real estate apps, websites, and systems.

These skill sets can be developed as a teen as you work on class, home, job, and volunteer assignments to prepare you to be successful in the real estate industry.

Even as a teenager, I was impressed by my dad being the man in charge of the building we lived in. But before he owned real estate, he was already a boss. My dad started off managing real estate for his uncle, who was a real estate attorney. In essence, he was a property manager. All properties require someone to manage them, whether it is the owner or someone else who is paid to do so. Whether you manage property for yourself or hire others, it important that you understand the role and responsibilities of a property manager.

The role of a property manager is a boss who supervises and manages the day-to-day activities of a real estate property. The basic responsibilities of a property manager may include, but are not limited to:

» Ensuring the property is always clean, safe, and sanitary

» Collecting rental money from tenants, with a system for all tenants to submit payments the same way. Key: Always provide customers with receipts for their payments for tracking purposes.

» Responding to tenant questions, concerns, and requests for repairs

» Preparing and advertising vacant units that are ready to be rented

» Interviewing and hiring staff and contractors

» Assigning maintenance workers to repair tasks

» Maintaining records and filing systems

» Providing status reports to the owner(s) to keep them updated about any changes with the property

» Paying bills associated with the property, such as lawn care, snow removal, and repairs

» Managing the finances for the property and creating financial reports to track the income and expenses (see Chapter 6 for more details)

The level of responsibility to manage someone else's property may vary depending on the owner's needs, and there should be an agreement in writing reflecting the specific tasks and pay rate. Nevertheless, the goal of any property manager should be to prioritize the best interests of the property owner by recommending, implementing, and overseeing the most efficient systems and processes to maintain the property in the best condition for profitability.

I am a strong believer and witness that a person who can be faithful in managing someone's property with integrity and excellence is a key to unlocking opportunities of success to purchasing and managing their own. There is a Bible scripture that says, *"And if you have not been trustworthy with someone else's property, who will give you property of your own?"* (Luke 16:12, NIV). My dad was faithful over managing other people's property which helped him to successfully obtain and maintain his own property.

Even at your age and stage in life, you don't need a boss title to have a boss mentality and behavior. Strive to develop the qualities and skills of a next-level boss now so you can take advantage of next-level opportunities in the next stage of your life.

Teen boss, who got the keys?

CHAPTER FIVE

ONE KEY UNLOCKS MANY DOORS

Careers in Real Estate

CHAPTER

5

I remember career day in high school, when we had the opportunity to learn about various career fields and their responsibilities. However, I don't recall ever seeing a real estate agent at those school events, yet real estate is the one key that opens many doors of opportunities. The real estate industry provides unlimited and multiple sources of income. The thing I love the most about real estate is the various careers and opportunities within that one profession that you can pursue to generate multiple streams of income. However, I realize that some people may aspire to work in other career fields. The great news is that you can still be a doctor, lawyer, teacher, or whatever you desire, while producing multiple sources of income through real estate within or outside of your career field. Whether you decide to work full time or part time, there are various professions within the real estate industry to take advantage of, with no limit on the amount of income you can make. Each profession has different roles, responsibilities, and qualifications as follows:

Real estate investor: Invests in real estate to make money. The investor may buy property individually or with others. The investor completes various financial and property analyses to determine how profitable a property is before they decide to spend their money and time on it.

Real estate agent or broker: A licensed individual who works to help others to buy, sell, or rent out a property. The real estate agent helps to negotiate deals and monitor the process to help their client(s) to get to the closing stage, which is the final step to transfer ownership or leasing of a property. To be a real estate agent or broker (different states use different titles), you must have an active real estate license in the state you desire to work in. To obtain a license, you must complete some classes and pass a test, as well as state and federal exams. The qualifications and requirements for a license may vary by state.

Property manager (landlord): Manages properties for themselves and/or others. The responsibilities of a property manager may vary depending on the agreement between the owner and the person or company hired to oversee the property (see Chapter 3 for details). A written property management agreement should be in place to ensure everyone is on the same page. However, the landlord may or may not be the owner of the property. The qualifications and licensing requirements to manage properties for others may vary by state.

Leasing agent: An individual who is licensed to help owners to rent out their properties and others to find properties to rent out. Leasing agents have limited capacities, in which they can only help with the renting of properties. In some states, such as Illinois, leasing agents can only help to rent out residential properties.

Managing brokers: Real estate agents who are licensed to manage a real estate office and other agents. However, designated managing brokers actually manage a real estate office and supervise other agents within that company. You must work as a real estate agent for a certain timeframe before you qualify to become a managing broker. Not all managing brokers operate in that capacity, as some just hold the license. The requirements and qualifications may vary by state.

Sponsoring broker: A real estate company that real estate agents and managing brokers must work under to hold their license. In some cases, the company may have a physical office you can walk into, or it may operate completely online. The main owner of a real estate company must hold a certain type of real estate license. However, the owner(s) may hire a managing broker to oversee their office(s). This may vary by state. Owners should seek the advice of an accountant and real estate attorney to determine the best business structure for their company.

Lender: A person or company that loans money to purchase, repair, or rehab a property. Each lender has different requirements to qualify for different loan types. The lender will charge you fees and interest for the money that you borrow. Be sure to know all of the stipulations and rules to borrow money from a lender.

Real estate attorney: Specializes in the legal aspects of the real estate transaction. Some states do not use real estate attorneys in the homebuying process, while it is highly recommended to utilize a real estate attorney in other states. It's important to hire an attorney who specializes in real estate to ensure your paperwork is accurate and to help make your homebuying process go as smooth as possible.

Appraiser: A licensed professional who assesses a property to determine its value. Lenders require appraisal reports to be completed on a property for sale to ensure the property is worth the price that the buyer is requesting a loan to buy it for.

Home inspector: A licensed professional that thoroughly examines the entire property to evaluate its condition. For example, the inspector will look at the plumbing, heating, and electrical systems at a property to ensure that they operate properly. The home inspector will provide a written report with photos about the results from their inspection. It is highly recommended to have a home inspection before you purchase a property.

Investor

Agent

Manager

"You can earn unlimited & multiple sources of income within the real estate industry!"

Lender

Inspector

Attorney

Real estate developer: Plans and creates ideas for new real estate developments or for renovating existing real estate. Developers are trained and understand the required state and city codes and regulations to build certain real estate within certain communities. Many developers are also architects or work with architects to draw a detailed design of the new real estate developments for the approval of the city or village in which the property is located.

General contractor (GC): The main licensed labor worker who oversees a building project at a construction site. The GC will get required permits from the city or village to repair, build, and/or update a property while monitoring the progress of their team of specialized contractors for the electricity, plumbing, heating, carpentry, and cooling (HVAC) systems needed to finish the project.

Insurance agent: Provides homeowners insurance or rental insurance. Insurance is important to have so that if there is damage, loss, and/or theft to your property and/or personal property, you can be reimbursed, as opposed to having to pay the full cost yourself to repair or replace something. Be sure to always check with more than one insurance company to compare their prices and what's covered in your insurance plan.

Real estate instructor: A person who teaches real estate courses on various real estate topics; they may also write lesson plans and curriculum for the classes. There are pre-licensing and continuing education (CE) real estate instructors. Pre-licensing instructors can teach the classes required to obtain and keep a real estate license in addition to other continuing education courses. However, a licensed CE instructor can only teach limited continuing education courses. In essence, the type of teaching license you have determines what type of real estate classes you are allowed to teach. This may vary by state.

The qualifications and processes for licensing for each real estate profession may vary by state; therefore, it is important to research the state you desire to work in. The great news is that there are no limits on how many roles you can work within the real estate industry at the same time, within different states, which provides the opportunity to diversify your sources of income. I mentioned earlier that I am a licensed instructor, managing broker, property manager, investor, and owner of my real estate company R' Legacy Realty. As such, I am using the one key of real estate to earn money from five different professions within the same field at the same time.

Now, who got the key that unlocks many doors to unlimited and multiple streams of income?

CHAPTER SIX

OWNERSHIP MINDSET
The Business of Real Estate

CHAPTER

6

Mind over matter is powerful! Before I actually became a property owner as a young adult, I first envisioned myself owning property as a teenager. While I did not know how, because I didn't have access to books like this, I just knew that I would get the keys to unlock the doors to my own property one day. Being exposed to my parents owning and managing different properties throughout my younger years developed an ownership mindset in me at a young stage, and I couldn't shake off what I saw and heard. My hope is that this book is just as impactful to you and helps you to develop an ownership mindset as well.

While I understand that everyone has different circumstances in life, and there may be a time in your life where you have to rent for a season, you should still have the mindset and faith that you will secure the keys of homeownership to real estate one day. Remember, homeowners have a median net worth 40 times higher than renters (Survey of Consumer Finances, Federal Reserves September 2020). In essence, your financial status is much higher as a homeowner than as a renter, especially as you pay off your mortgage loan on the property you own. Be determined to own real estate, whether it's just the house you reside in or several properties that others live or conduct business in – be an owner.

We often see people brag on social media about being a boss, and it's an honor to be in a leadership position. But know that bosses are not all necessarily owners, yet all owners are bosses who have the mindset as such. For example, a real estate agent is a boss who sets

DID YOU KNOW?

"

HOMEOWNERS
have net worth
40x
HIGHER
than
RENTERS

- Federal Reserves 2020

"

$

$

Renter's
Net Worth

Homeowner's
Net Worth

their own hours and manages their own schedule and customers, and a managing broker is a boss who supervises real estate agents and manages a real estate office. But a sponsoring broker is both a boss and the owner of the real estate office that real estate agents and managing brokers work under. As a real estate investor, you are a business owner: your business is the selling or renting of real estate for the exchange of money to make a profit. As a real estate business owner, the property you own is your product, and you provide some level of customer service to those who may rent or buy your property.

But it is not enough to have a thought about becoming an owner without a written plan of execution. *"Write the vision, and make it plain"* (Habakkuk 2:2, KJV). Aspiring business owners in all industries should have a business plan, which is a roadmap of how your business will operate to make a profit. The business plan includes the details of your products and services, the team, the marketing plan, and the financial plan. Below are the components of a business plan:

» **Executive Summary:** A summary of your business plan with the main keys from each section. Generally, you write this section last, though it is the first part of your business plan.

» **Business Description:** A detailed description of your company, which should include the concept of your company, your company goals, accomplishments, the mission statement (the purpose of your business) and the vision statement (what you intend to happen in the future).

» **Organization:** Details about your team members, partnerships, processes, and systems. Remember, a next-level boss understands the importance of teams because teamwork effectively makes the dream work.

» **Marketing Plan:** A strategy for how you will communicate the value of your product/service to the public, particularly your customers. The marketing plan includes:

- o Description of your business industry (real estate)

- o Identification of your target market (your primary and secondary customers)

- o S.W.O.T analysis: Strengths, weaknesses, opportunities, and threats of your company versus your competition. This is important to identify what other companies are doing well and areas of improvement for your company. Also, a SWOT analysis can help you figure out what makes your different from your competitors, also known as your niche or competitive advantage.

- o Marketing strategy regarding your product, price, place and promotion, known as the marketing mix.

» **Financial Plan:** A breakdown of the money that your company projects and actually makes (revenue/income) and spends (expenses). The financial plan should include various financial reports such as a budget, cash flow statement, income statement, and balance sheet over a certain period of time such as a month, quarter, or one or more years.

- o Budget: Projection of the income and expenses from your business.

- o Income statement: Report of the actual breakdown of the income and expenses from your business.

- o Balance sheet: Report of your company's assets (things

that add value, such as real estate) versus liabilities (things that take away value, such as a mortgage payment) to determine the equity (assets minus liabilities).

o Cash Flow: Report of the actual cash that flows in and out of the company each month. This is the most important statement because it tells you how much cash the company has on hand.

The financial reporting of a business is often the most intimidating component for business owners, yet I believe it is the most important, because without money, there is no business, just an idea or charity. Therefore, I highly recommend that you invest in financial literacy classes to better understand financial reports in advance. While you may decide to hire a financial coach or accountant in the future, it's still important to understand and know how to effectively manage money for yourself to avoid being taken advantage of.

A well-thought-out business plan helps you to reduce as much risk as possible, as every aspect of the company affects its ability to be profitable. The plan may change as the needs of the customers and the industry changes; you must adjust appropriately to maintain success and expand. I recommend that you seek the counsel of an attorney and accountant to decide the best business structure for your company.

With an ownership mindset and business strategies, you have all the keys that you need at this stage of life to get started with your real estate career. Future owner, who got the keys? Affirm it with confidence, "I got the keys," because now it's time to use them.

CHAPTER SEVEN

USE YOUR KEY
How to Get Started NOW

CHAPTER

7

Who got the keys? You got the keys! If you've read this entire book, you now have the keys of information to unlock a plan of action to prepare to become a successful real estate owner one day. "But I'm just a teen," you might be saying. No worries, it is never too early to prepare to build wealth through real estate. Remember, it's a mindset first! Below are the steps to use your keys to get started NOW. Please be sure to include your parent(s)/guardian(s) in the process.

1. **Write out your real estate goals.** Goals are important to help you create a roadmap of your success. Your goals should be SMART: specific, measurable, achievable, realistic, and timely. For each goal, write the plan of action to achieve it, the resources needed, and the time frame to complete it. It's okay if your goals change over time; you must start somewhere. I recommend you have a trusted adult to help you with your goals and to help monitor your progress in reaching your desired outcomes.

2. **Continue to be a student of the industry.** The more informed you are, the better decisions you can make to avoid a lot of financial hardships and setbacks. I applaud you for empowering yourself by reading this book. However, the industry is always going to change, like any business, so it is important that you are always aware of the current trends and systems of real estate. Invest and take financial literacy, business, and real estate classes continuously. If there is a

certain field or specialty of real estate that attracts you most, take more classes in that area. There are many free classes online and books in the library.

3. **Speak daily affirmations.** Your words have power to manifest your reality. No matter how you feel, don't let fear stop you, speak positive words over your current and future circumstances. Specifically, use my free daily affirmations that came with this book called *Affirmations to Build Generational Wealth*. The affirmations will help you to declare and further develop an ownership mindset and determination to build a legacy of wealth for you and your family through real estate.

4. **Shadow the homebuying process.** If a trusted adult in your family is buying real estate, ask your parents if you can go house shopping with them and ask lots of questions. Also, try to go to the home inspection with them. In addition to learning more about assessing the quality of a property, you may grow to love the job of a home inspector. Shadowing the homebuying process will give you a better understanding of what you have learned from this book.

5. **Start saving now.** Whether you receive birthday or Christmas money, a paycheck, an allowance, or any money from others, make a habit of saving a portion of it. This single habit can allow you to avoid most financial challenges in the future. Start to save ten percent of whatever money you bring in. If that is too much, start at five percent and work your way up to ten – the goal is to build up the habit of saving now. You will be excited about how much money is accumulated from saving in the future. Ask a trusted adult to set up a savings account for you at a bank to hold the money for you. The money in a savings account should only be used for emergencies or your purpose for building up the savings.

6. **Become an intern for a real estate company.** Whether you are serving as a volunteer or on a paid basis, with the permission of your parent/guardian, connect with a real estate professional or company for mentorship, experience, and hands-on skills to be successful in the real estate industry. Often companies need help with secretarial duties such as organizing files and documents, answering calls, and especially with daily posts on their social media pages.

7. **Utilize my workbook.** The *Who Got the Keys?* Workbook includes hands-on activities and case studies of real-life scenarios to better equip and engage the entire family in their goal to build wealth through real estate generationally. The workbook is a great way for you to assess what you learned from this book. You can find a copy at www.whogotthekeys.com.

8. **Pass the keys.** Commit to building generational wealth within your family and community members by sharing this book of knowledge with your peers, younger siblings, cousins, and friends. Some may take the keys of information, while others may resist them, but as long as you offer this information to others, you have done your part. It's a generational thang, and next-level bosses know the importance of passing the keys on to help others elevate themselves as well.

9. **Apply for a real estate scholarship.** Do you want to become a real estate agent? It's possible! In some states, you can become a real estate agent at the age of 18 with a high school diploma or GED. The age and cost to obtain a real estate license may vary by state, as well as the required classes. Research online real estate scholarships in your state for funding opportunities to take the real estate classes. Many real estate associations and states have funds specifically for minorities such as the

National Association of Real Estate Brokers (NAREB) and the National Association of Realtors.

JOHN P. ROGERS

Real Estate Foundation

My siblings and I started the John P. Rogers Real Estate Foundation to honor our father, who gave us the keys to real estate investing. We will continue his legacy by providing scholarships to black teens to obtain a real estate license. If you reside in Illinois or Indiana, are between the ages of 18 and 19, and have obtained a high school diploma or GED, you may be eligible for a scholarship. For more information, visit www.whogotthekeys.com or www.rlegacyrealty.com.

10. **Celebrate your wins and learn from your losses.** There is so much a person can accomplish in the real estate industry, so it is easy to compare your level of success to others. Remember to be true to your purpose and real estate journey. For every goal you set and accomplish, be sure to celebrate yourself. The fact that you have completed this book is a win, as it means you are already ahead of your time! Yes, there will be unexpected setbacks and losses along the way. But even those are keys of opportunity to learn lessons to do it right and better the next time around. Whatever you do, don't give up!

No longer do you have to stand outside the door knocking and waiting for someone to let you in. Now you have keys to allow yourself in to create wealth for yourself and the generations after you.

This is the key that I give my real estate clients to celebrate and take pictures with when they secure the actual keys to their new property. Now, I am giving you this key to applaud you on securing the keys of information to build wealth through real estate by completing this book!

Congratulations, young wealth builder!

www.whogotthekeys.com

www.rlegacyrealty.com

IG: @realtordonnajr

FB: facebook.com/realtordonnajr

REFERENCES

Allaway, Wellington J., Fillmore W. Galaty, Robert C. Kyle. *Modern Real Estate Practice in Illinois*, edited by Leo Schwartz and Martha R. Williams, JD, 10th ed Wisconsin Dearborn Real Estate Education, 2020.

Anderson, Dana, "Redlining Legacy of Inequity: $212,000 Less Home Equity, Low Homeownership Rates for Black Families," Redfin, June 11, 2020, www.redfin.com/news.

Aronowitz, Michelle, Jung Choi, Edward Golding, Morgan Green, Richard Green, Maurice Jourdain-Earl, Ashlyn A. Nelson, Vanessa Gail Perry, Lisa Rice, Lauren Rhue. "2020 State Of Housing In Black America: Challenges Facing Black Homeowners And Homebuyers During The Covid-19 Pandemic And An Agenda For Public Policy," NAREB, August 2020, https://www.nareb.com/shiba-report/.

Bhutta, Neil, Andrew C. Chang, Lisa J. Dettling, and Joanne W. Hsu (2020). "Disparities in Wealth by Race and Ethnicity in the 2019 Survey of Consumer Finances," FEDS Notes. Washington: Board of Governors of the Federal Reserve System, September 28, 2020, https://doi.org/10.17016/2380-7172.2797.

Choi, Jung Hyun, "Breaking Down the Black-White Homeownership Gap," Urban Wire (blog), Urban Institute, February 21, 2020, https://www.urban.org/urban-wire/breaking-down-black-white-homeownership-gap.

"Data USA: Real Estate Brokers and Sales Agents." *Deloitte.com.* The Census Bureau's American Community Survey (ACS) Public Use Microdata Sample (PUMS), 2017 Web. 12 January 2021. https://

datausa.io/profile/soc/real-estate-brokers-sales-agents#ethnicity

Gates Jr., Henry Louis. "The African American Many Rivers to Cross: The Truth Behind 40 Acres and a Mule," PBS, 2013, https://www.pbs.org/wnet/african-americans-many-rivers-to-cross/history/the-truth-behind-40-acres-and-a-mule/.

Lockwood, Beatrix. "The History of Redlining." ThoughtCo, Dec. 16, 2020, thoughtco.com/redlining-definition-4157858.

"Quarterly Residential Vacancies and Homeownership: Fourth Quarter 2020." *Census.gov*. US Census Bureau, US Department of Commerce, 2021 Web. 7 Feb. 2021. https://www.census.gov/housing/hvs/index.html

Creative Production Credits

Made in the USA
Monee, IL
11 March 2021